Published in the United States of America by The Child's World®
PO Box 326 • Chanhassen, MN 55317-0326
800-599-READ • www.childsworld.com

My First Steps to Math™ is a registered trademark of Scholastic, Inc.

Library of Congress Cataloging-in-Publication Data
Moncure, Jane Belk.
My five book / by Jane Belk Moncure.
p. cm. — (My first steps to math)
ISBN 1-59296-660-8 (lib. bdg. : alk. paper)
1. Counting—Juvenile literature. 2. Number concept—Juvenile literature. I. Title.
QA113.M663 2006
513.2'11—dc22
2005025695

My five Book

by Jane Belk Moncure

illustrated by Kate Flanagan

This is Little five.

Little  lives in the house of five.

It has five rooms. Count them.

Every day Little  goes for a walk.

One day he goes into his garden.
He finds some carrots. How many?

As he pulls up the carrots,
five rabbits hop by.

He gives each rabbit a carrot.

The rabbits eat the carrots.
Then they say, "Let's play tag."
Little  plays with them.

"I will catch you," he says.

"No!" say the rabbits.

They hop down a rabbit hole.
How many are left?

The sun is hot. Little  is hot, too.

"I know how to get cool," he says.
He hops five hops to the beach.

Then he takes off two shoes,

two socks,

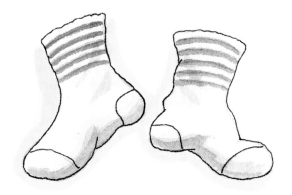

and one pair of overalls.

How many things does Little  take off?

Then Little  makes a sand castle and puts shells on it. How many?

Just then some little crabs run by. How many?

"I will catch you," says Little  five .
But he slips in the sand.

Some crabs hide in the sand castle.
How many are left?

Little  goes wading.

He sees one sea star on a rock.

He picks up the sea star and counts its arms.
How many?

"You have more arms than I do," he says.

Just then, more sea stars climb up on the rock. How many?

The little sea star in his hand is sad.

So Little  puts him back in the water.

How many sea stars wave good-bye?

Little  five hops on down the beach.

He finds a boat,

two oars,

a fishing net,

and a fishing rod.

How many things does he find?

Then Little  puts on his clothes to go fishing.

How many fish swim past?

"Whee!" says he.
"One fish for me!"

How many fish are left?

"Whee!" says he. "Two fish for me!"

How many fish are left?

"Now I have three," says he.

How many fish are left?

Then Little  catches two more fish!

"Five fat fish for me," says he.

But the fish are sad.

"I will let you go," says Little 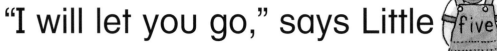 five .

How many fish swim away?

How many are left?

"You must go, too," he says.

And the last fish does.

How many fish jump for joy?

Little  found five of everything.

five carrots

five rabbits

five crabs

five sea stars

five fish

Now you find five things.

Let's add with Little .

 +  =

5 + 0 = 5

  =

3 + 2 = 5

Now take away.

5   –   1   =   4

5   –   0   =   5

Little 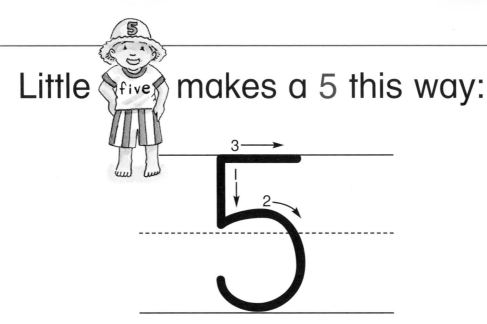 makes a 5 this way:

Then he makes the number word like this:

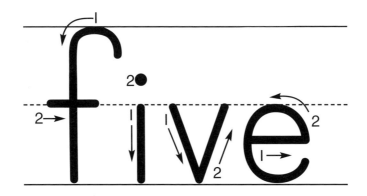

You can make them in the air with your finger.